Maria Never Gives Up

ARE YOU BRAVE LIKE ME?

A Story About A Child With A Chronic Illness

Mary Baliker

Maria Never Gives Up

design by:

Pretty Good

PRINTMAKING

www.amazon.com

Acknowledgments

I am dedicating this book to my Dad for helping me see my story was important to write. Throughout my life, he has provided me support and mentorship. Most importantly, he has reminded me to follow my dreams.

I thank, and admire, my mom for her indefatigable love and companionship during the best and worst of times.

With gratitude I thank my brother, Doug, who selflessly gave me the gift of life by donating one of his kidneys to me. My champion!

My deepest thanks to my friend, Holly Helscher, for her enormous help with writing this book. I was wasting so much time figuring out just what to say, how to organize the book and stay on schedule. She helped complete the book. And made it fun!

I'd also like to thank the following for reading the manuscript, filling in details and making suggestions: Jim Baliker (my husband), Jean Fregin (my Mom), Robert Frankenstein (my Dad), Holly Helscher, Marleen Ash, and Kathy Schultz.

To my Mom & Dads, Jeanne, Robert, and Marty, the best parents. I couldn't have made this journey without each of you by my side every step of the way.

To Jim, my best friend and the love of my life!

To my dog, Kona, who sat by my side while I wrote. He kept me company into the wee hours of the mornings.

To my family, Doug, Sue, Matt, Amanda, Megan, Tristen, Trynia, Godric, Wynter, Gabe, Bill, Lorraine, Joan, Jim, Paul, Dave, Steve, Pam, Aja, Diane, Curt, Linda, Chris, Rich, Wally, Melody, Ron, Gavin, and Sandy, I love you!

To all my family and friends. You are all so special to me.

To all the medical team at the University of Wisconsin Hospital who made this book possible.

To my brother, Doug, to my donor and donor families.

You are all heroes!

Foreward

A while back a friend of mine, Tammy, came to me and said, "I'm taking a month off work because I'm donating one of my kidneys." Tammy had an older daughter, so I immediately thought the worst. But her daughter was fine. Tammy was a match for someone on the organ donor list and was following through on an open-ended promise she'd made as an organ donor. I thought, "Wow! What an amazing act of courage."

Little did I know that years later I'd meet someone even more courageous. That person, Mary Baliker, is the author of this book. She developed kidney disease at a very young age – nine years old. At the time transplants weren't possible for children.

We met through a mutual friend in my writing critique group. Mary needed a reader and I raised my virtual hand. I'll always remember the subject line of the email that introduced us. We have a reader!

When I finished reading Mary's draft, I knew I wanted to help her get it published. It's a story that will resonate with children, their parents, and even adults who live their lives with kidney disease.

A unique feature about Mary's, story is it's told through the eyes of her teddy bear. Teddy introduces us to his BFF, Mary (named Maria in the story) and we become a part of her life. We meet her before the diagnosis of kidney disease. Then we walk with her through the fears and challenges of having it.

Mary is a living testimonial to the concept that bravery isn't an absence of fear. It's being terrified and doing what you need to do anyway. When you're nine, that's a tough call. When you're a teenager it's even tougher. The last thing a teen wants is to be different. But Mary was different. Living with the idea of death every day forces a difference.

Maria Never Gives Up shares the emotions of Mary's jagged path. The book isn't about the clinical diagnosis and prognosis. It's about hope, and lack of hope coexisting in the same person. Mary and her family learned how to balance the two disparate feelings.

The book normalizes the conflicting emotions existing in children and parents facing the same, or similar situation. It gives people permission to be scared. Permission to cry. And even permission to laugh.

Mary's first doctor gave her less than one year to live. Nevertheless, she defied all the odds. She went into remission long enough for medical science and research to catch up. By the time Mary was 17, transplants for children didn't carry as much risk. That's when Mary's brother, Doug, donated his own kidney to her. It was a heroic moment for both of them. Unfortunately it wasn't Mary's last transplant. Over her life she's had a few others, but come through them with the courage she portrayed when she was nine.

Perhaps my friend, Tammy, was one of Mary's donors. I have no idea, but I like to think the world is that small – and that awesome.

Holly Helscher, *Ph.D.*
Owner, *Information Marketing to Businesses*
Cincinnati, Ohio

Preface

Mary wrote this children's book in hope that it will help other children in their struggle with a health crisis.

Mary's illness inspired her to become a Healthcare Advocate, which she has been most of her adult life. Mary's professional work experience over the past thirty years includes working with many health care organizations. This includes the University of Wisconsin School of Medicine & Public Health, Affinity Strategies LLC., Patient Centered Outcomes Research Institute, the Department of Defense Congressionally Directed Medical Research Program, Astellas Pharma Inc., and Long Beach Memorial Hospital.

She has worked as an Organ Procurement Coordinator, Clinical Research Transplant Coordinator, Outreach Transplant Education Coordinator, Transplant Ambassador, Grant Writer and Reviewer, Healthcare Administration in Asthma, Pulmonary Disease, and Carbone Cancer Center. Currently she works as a healthcare consultant, as well as a inspirational speaker educating and informing attendees with her stories and personal experience.

Mary has also been a patient advocate, and been involved in legislative work. She currently serves on the United Network for Organ Sharing (Patient Affairs Committee), UW Health Patient and Family Advisory Committees, Friends of UW Heath Board of Directors, National Kidney Foundation (Peer Mentor), National Kidney Foundation (Kidney Advocacy Committee), Midwest Kidney Network Board of Directors (ESRD Network 11), and National Patient/Family Engagement Learning & Action Network Health Services Advisory Group.

Table of Contents

Introduction to My Journey

Hi, my name is Teddy. I'm a teddy bear and I belong to a little girl named Maria. I'm kind of scraggly looking because she takes me everywhere.

Once she spilled some red juice on my left paw.

"Oh, Teddy, I'm so sorry," she said. Then she raced to the bathroom to get a cloth wet to clean it. She wiped it until all that was left was a light red stain.

Another time Maria's dog, Peppy, played with me. He grabbed two of the three blue buttons on my plaid vest. They popped off. He then scooted them around with his nose like they were hockey pucks. Then he scooted them right down the heat vent.

Maria rushed into her bedroom where she knew she had a flashlight. She shined it into the vent, but couldn't see either button. They were lost forever.

"Bad, Peppy," she said to the dog wagging her finger in front of his nose. *"Don't do it again."* All Peppy did was hang out his tongue.

She snatched me up and jogged into where her mother was sewing. Her mother loved to sew.

"Mom," Maria said presenting me to her. *"Can you sew more blue buttons on Teddy's vest?"*

Maria's mother looked through her glass jar of buttons.

"I don't have any blue ones. I don't even have two of the same color. Why don't you pick two you like and I'll sew them on. Teddy will have to be happy with mismatched buttons. It'll make him a very interesting bear, won't it?"

Maria picked out a dark brown button, like the color of a tree trunk. The other one was sunflower yellow. After that, Maria always made sure Peppy couldn't play with me.

My fur is the color of chocolate. I have pink peeking out of my ears. They match my pink and blue bow tie.

Because she takes me everywhere with her, I travel a lot. Sometimes it's in a car. Other times it's in a baby carriage with kittens. Mostly I travel in Maria's backpack.

My favorite thing to do is snuggle with Maria at night where it's warm and safe. My next favorite thing is sharing secrets with her. I know more about Maria than anyone.

The most important thing about me is Maria. She always tells me, "**You're my best friend, ever! I can tell you anything**." And she does.

Today I'm going to tell you a story about when Maria was the most scared she's ever been. She was more scared than she was the one time she rode a huge roller coaster at the state fair. Or the time she rode a wagon on a haunted hayride on Halloween.

She was terrified because she was sick. It wasn't the kind of sick that keeps you home from school and you miss a spelling test. It was the kind of sick when the doctor says, "**You have to go to the hospital so we can figure out how to make you well**." Has this ever happened to you?

If so, I know you talked to your parents. Terrible ideas probably fill up your head late at night when everyone sleeps. Maybe you feel like exploding. A special friend like me is important during those times. Under the covers that night Maria whispered everything to me. If you have a special friend like me, you can whisper everything about how petrified you are.

If this kind of illness is happening to you right now, I know you're confused. I know you feel different than everyone else. Those feelings are worse if you have to go to the hospital in an ambulance. Or in one of those medical helicopters you might see on television sometimes. You know it's serious. You feel helpless. Maybe a little hopeless.

It's okay to be frightened and worried. I learned it when all this happened to Maria. Grown up people are afraid when they have to go to the hospital, too. There are lots of people we don't usually see. You don't know anyone. You've never seen any of the big machines that perform all the tests the doctors order. Even though everything is explained ahead of time, you really don't know what's going to happen. Plus, nothing looks like home. It can be terrifying.

I learned another big secret, too. If you're so sick you have to go to a hospital, being afraid is normal. Really normal. Talking about how you feel helps. If this is happening to you, be sure you talk about it.

When Maria had to go to the hospital, she took me with her. She talked to me all the time. That's why I know so much about her story and what happened to her.

Are you ready to find out about Maria's story? It has some scary parts. It has some funny parts, too. Even though this story is about Maria, she wants me telling it to help you. Through her story, you're going to love her as much as I do.

The Child in All of Us
Chapter 1

Everything I'm about to tell you happened to Maria when she was nine years old. She was like lots of little girls everywhere. She had curly light brown hair. When she wore it short, it flipped up on the edges. Most days her mother would put barrettes in her hair. It seemed like she always lost one by the end of the day.

Lots of kids live in the city. Other kids live in the country. Maria lived in both places. When she was in second grade, her parents got divorced. She and her brother, Doug, lived in the city, called Beaver Dam. Their dad stayed on the hobby farm where they'd all lived before the divorce.

Hobby farms aren't like dairy farms that supply milk to grocery stores. Or cattle farms that supply meat to those same stores.

A hobby farm is a farm people have because they love it. Maria and Doug loved it more than anyone. That's why they were there so much of the time, even after the divorce.

When they were on the farm, on nice days, Maria would grab me and say, *"Let's go swing!"* More often she said, *"Let's explore the mysterious woods today."*

She called them mysterious because she never knew what she'd find in them.

The woods bordered the hobby farm and had lots of trails running through them. When Maria played explorer, she tucked me into a backpack. My head always peeped out the top so I could see where we went.

She scrambled along, her head down glancing from side-to-side as she looked for treasures on the ground.

"Look at this feather! I think it's from a blue jay," she'd announce. Then she'd shove it in her backpack.

Or she'd say, *"Here's a green stone with sparkles."* That would go into the backpack, too.

She jumped, danced and shouted at her best find. *"An arrowhead. My collection is growing again."* Collecting arrowheads was one of Maria's hobbies.

When she wasn't exploring, we'd sit in her room, or sometimes on the porch reading. Every so often she'd look up from her book. *"The girl in this book lives in Japan. I want to see Japan, don't you? I want to travel all over the world with you."* Then she would add Japan to her list of places to visit.

She even made a game about it. We'd play it in the woods. *"I'm a famous explorer, like Christopher Columbus. Today we're going to France."* Then she'd take a stick and wave it like a magic wand. That transformed all of the woods into France. Other days it was Spain, or Ireland, or Canada. When it was France, one of the tallest trees became the Eiffel Tower. It had the best branches for climbing. We climbed up to the top every time.

Other times Maria pretended to be a zoo explorer. On those days she'd say, *"My job is to find new animals for the zoo."* Then we'd find new animals. Once we saw a raccoon and imagined it was a living dinosaur.

We roamed around with baby foxes, chattering squirrels and burping frogs. Even though she was a made-up zookeeper bringing animals back to a zoo, she'd say, *"We're going to leave them in nature."* It looked like a zoo without cages.

Maria's favorite animal was the butterfly. She liked darting around with them. She loved trying to see how close she could get to one before it flew away. If she spied one on a flower, she'd tiptoe up to it step-by-step. She never cracked any sticks lying on the ground, or crunched any dead leaves left over from last fall. I thought that was a miracle.

She liked butterflies so much she checked out a book at the library to learn more about them. When she'd spot their cocoons in the yard, she checked on them every day. "*I hope this butterfly comes out today,*" she'd say to her dad, "*when I'm standing right there. I want to see what kind of butterfly comes out.*" If she timed it just right, she'd see the butterfly's first flight. Then she'd become a butterfly, too, following it all over the yard. She never captured a single butterfly, though; because she was afraid it would die if she did.

When Maria fluttered along with the butterflies she'd make believe she was on an adventure around the world. She flew along the trails with the butterflies. On those days her dreams of world travel came true, at least for an afternoon. Then she'd read another book and add another city in the world she wanted to see.

When she wasn't playing, or doing homework, Maria had chores. Her favorite one was raising the baby animals that had no mothers. Many of them needed bottle-feeding.

"*I just love you,*" she'd say to Tiny, the baby lamb the neighbors had given them. Tiny was so small he fit in the crook of Maria's arm.

During feeding, Maria would kiss Tiny's nose and ask, "*Do you like your food?*" When the bottle was empty she'd play with Tiny for a while, and then trot her back to the barn, fetching the next baby animal that was hungry.

Besides the orphaned animals, the farm also had ducks and geese. They sprinted all over the farm yakking for attention. Maria and Doug did their best to love them, but they were feisty animals, impossible to hold and pet.

There were other special animals as well. An Appaloosa pony named Sudsy lived with them. He enjoyed being brushed. His favorite food was apples. When Maria offered apples to Sudsy, she always made sure she held her palm flat. Otherwise her fingers might get nicked.

At the farm Maria spent lots of time with her friend, Patricia. The two of them had known each other since they were 5 years old.

When they got together, the girls made up plays for their dolls to act out. Other times they rode bikes or played in the woods. The friends shared secrets like most friends do. One day I heard Maria tell Patricia, "*I really like Mike even though he's in the grade ahead of me. His freckles are really cute. Do you think he likes me?*"

Patricia crinkled up her nose, "*Yuck. Boys. Except for Steve. I like Steve.*"

"*Steve! He's weird. How can you like him?*" Maria punched Patricia's shoulder.

Then both girls laughed so hard they couldn't breathe.

When Maria wasn't hanging out with Patricia, she hung out with Mittens. Mittens was a white colored cat with polka dots of tan. And all four of her paws were tan, so it looked like she wore mittens all the time.

Mittens had babies or a litter of kittens every summer. Maria loved tucking all the kittens into her doll buggy. "**You need fresh air,**" she'd say to them as she pranced up and down the streets.

While they were kittens, they loved the rides. As they grew, they'd jump out and race away. Eventually they all got good at catching mice, and sleeping.

Both Maria and Doug felt warm and squishy about all kinds of animals. Even the ones that lived in the mysterious woods.

One winter when Maria visited her grandparents, she said, "**What if the woods animals can't find any food? Can we feed them like our other animals?**"

Her grandfather said, "**How about if I I give you a salt block? A salt block is the size of a basketball, only it's square. It sat under their biggest tree, near the trunk. Deer, squirrels, and even foxes liked it, only they didn't eat it. They licked it. The salt's not like the kind you use on your own food. It's more like vitamins for animals.**"

Like every kid, Maria and Doug started school in the fall when the leaves on the trees change from green to reds, yellows and oranges. Doug was a few years ahead of Maria. He liked reading, too, but his class didn't have a reading time during the day. Maria's class did. At least once a week she'd dance into the house and announce, "**I got another gold star!**"

"**What book did you finish this time?**" her mother asked.

"**Today I finished Charlotte's Web. It's my new favorite. That means I have 15 gold stars. I've read more books than anyone in the class. Reading is my very best favorite part of school.**"

Her mother would kiss her and say, "**Good job, sweetie.**"

Their mother fixed them an after-school snack while they told her about their day. Sometimes their snack would be cookies with milk. Other times it would be bread with peanut butter and jelly. Sometimes it was a cluster of grapes.

On Fridays they shoved their snacks into their mouths, they got to see their dad and the farm. If they didn't get there early enough, they'd miss feeding the animals.

Almost every Friday Maria shouted, "**Hurry up, Mom!**"

Her mother always laughed. "**I'll be there in a second,**" she'd say.

The half hour to the farm seemed like centuries. Maria bounced on the seat the whole drive. Her mother would say, "**Please sit still.**" Except Maria never would.

The minute they arrived, Maria shoved open her car door. Feeding the animals took about an hour. When all the feeding was done, it was time for their dinner.

Afterwards Maria and Doug watched a little television, or played outside. Before going to sleep each night, Maria read at least one chapter in a book.

The fall when she was nine, she was reading a Nancy Drew mystery, dreaming about having those same kinds of book adventures herself. Little did she know she might not be able to make those dreams come true.

Shattered Dreams
Chapter 2

Toward the end of every summer, Maria and Doug went school shopping with their dad. The summer Maria was nine-years-old was no exception.

During the shopping expedition, Maria's father scrunched up his brow and said to her, "*Are you feeling okay?*" He touched the top of her forehead with the back of his hand. "*You don't feel warm, so you must not have a fever.*"

"*I'm fine, Dad,*" Maria said. "*But I'm a little tired today.*"

When they got home to their mother, Maria flew to her room to tell me all about her new clothes. "*I'd give you a fashion show,*" she told me, "*but I'm tired. I think I'll take a nap before dinner.*" She snuggled up on the bed with me and closed her eyes.

It wasn't long before we both heard tapping on her bedroom door. Maria's mother peeked in. "*Hi, honey. Your dad tells me you're not feeling well. He thinks maybe you have a bug or something. What do you think?*"

Maria said, "*I'm fine except I'm tired.*"

Maria's mother sat on the edge of the bed and then put her palms on either side of Maria's face. "*Your cheeks seem a bit swollen. Do they hurt?*"

Maria shook her head.

"*Does anything hurt?*"

Again, Maria shook her head.

"*Your father seemed to think your stomach was a little swollen, too. He noticed it when some of the clothes didn't fit around your waist.*"

"*Mom,*" Maria said, "*I'm fine. I'm tired, that's all. Once I get some sleep, I'll be fine.*"

Maria's mother stood up. "*We'll see how you feel later.*"

Maria took her nap, and felt okay for the rest of the summer. But once school started, even Maria worried something was wrong.

Two weeks into the new school year, when Maria came home and crunched on her apple snack, she said, "*Mom, I'm really tired. I think I'll go to bed early tonight.*"

Her mother stopped peeling potatoes at the sink and turned toward Maria. "*Are you playing more at recess? Maybe games with more running?*"

Maria shrugged her shoulders up to her ears. "*Maybe, homework seems harder this year. And it's taking longer to finish. I think I'm not used to that.*"

Maria's mother pursed her lips and went back to peeling potatoes. All she said was, "*Hum.*"

A month into the school year Maria's teacher called and requested a conference with Maria's parents. It was scheduled for the very next day.

"*Is everything okay at home with Maria?*" Miss Lukens asked. "*She isn't playing at recess. She sits on the sidelines and watches, her eyes nearly shut. And she's falling asleep at her desk in the afternoons. She's not paying attention to the lessons and her homework isn't the best. Her grades are slipping. This isn't like Maria. Have you noticed anything at home?*"

Maria's mom nodded. Maria's mother spoke first, "*She complains about being tried and has been going to bed earlier and earlier.*"

The conference was short because no one really knew how to help Maria. On the ride home Maria's mom decided to get Maria checked out by the doctor. She made the appointment for the following week.

On the day the appointment arrived, Maria didn't have to go to school. She worried about getting her homework done, but her mother said, "It's fine. It's more important we find out why you're so tired."

After her checkup, Dr. Damon brought Maria and her mother into his office. Maria had never been in his office. It had a big desk and lots of pictures and framed diplomas on the wall.

"*I do think her stomach, ankles and cheeks are swollen,*" he said. "*And there are a few other things that seem out of the ordinary. I am referring her to the University of Wisconsin Children's' Hospital in Madison.*"

Maria's mother scooted up to the edge of her chair, "*Is she going to be okay?*"

Maria knew the tone she heard in her mother's voice. It was the kind of voice she used when one of the animals got hurt and she didn't know what to do.

"*Now, Mrs. Frank, we're going to get to the bottom of Maria's tiredness. I just don't have the equipment here to run all the tests we need. We'll find out faster with her in the hospital where all the equipment is.*"

"*How long before we know anything?*" Maria's mother asked.

Maria thought her heart would burst out of her chest. And it seemed as if she could hear it thump in her ears. That hadn't happened since she was a little kid and got lost in the grocery store. She wanted to bite her nails, but she knew her mother wouldn't like that. She knew that it wasn't ladylike.

She had a lot of questions. She wasn't brave enough to ask any of them except one. *"Can I bring Teddy with me?"* She lifted me up so the doctor could see me.

The doctor smiled at her. *"of course. A few tests take a little bit of time, so you'll be there overnight. Teddy will be a perfect friend to stay with you."*

The next day Maria and her parents were on their way to the University of Wisconsin Children's Hospital in Madison, about an hour away. Doug stayed with their grandparents.

Even though Maria knew hospitals were big, when they drove into the parking lot, it seemed like it was as big as hundred houses all put together.

It took forever to check in and get her to her room. She wasn't allowed to wear her own nightgown. She had to wear one they gave her.

As soon as she was settled, two nurses came in and wheeled her whole bed to another place in the hospital. Her mother followed along side, but I got to ride along with Maria. Except that she squeezed me so hard I couldn't breathe very well. Her mother didn't notice, but I could see her bottom lip quivering. She sucked it into her mouth. I knew that meant she was trying hard to be brave.

The room had a gigantic machine in it. It kind of looked like a thermos bottle lying on its side. And it was so big, it seemed like five Maria's could fit inside. *"Maria,"* one of the nurses said. *"We're going to do a test called a CT Scan. CT is the short name for computed tomography."*

Maria scrunched up her nose. *"Do I have to remember the whole name?"*

The nurse smiled and shook her head. "No. But I do need you to drink this liquid. After a few minutes we'll slide you into the CT machine and take some pictures of your heart and your tummy."

"What does the drink do?" Maria asked. She squinted at the white liquid as if she didn't trust it. Which she didn't.

"The color of it is a contrast to the color of the lining of your heart and tummy. It's like you would draw a picture on colored paper. Then you'd outline the picture in black so you could see it better on the colored paper."

"Oh." Maria took a sip. *"Yuck! It's doesn't taste good."* She stuck out her tongue and wiped it.

"You're right. It tastes terrible. But you'll have to be brave and drink all of it. And don't give any to your teddy bear, okay?"

"Can I hold my nose when I drink it?"

The nurse laughed and patted Maria's shoulder. *"Yes, that's fine."*

Maria couldn't take me with her inside the machine, so she gave me to her mom. But later Maria told me she felt alone and separated from everything in the whole world.

It seemed to Maria the CT scan might have been easier than all the blood tests. They stuck needles in her arm and took out blood every few hours. It reminded Maria of her mother's apple-shaped pincushion when she was sewing. Needles went in and out of it all the time. Except blood didn't come out with them.

Maria cried when those nurses came around because she was really scared of needles.

"You'll get used to it," her mother told her.

"No, I won't," Maria said. *"Why do they have to do any of this?"*

"The more they know about what's going on inside you, the more they'll know how to fix it."

In the middle of all the blood tests, Maria also had to do something called a 24-hour urine test. That one didn't hurt, but peeing inside a large plastic cup felt weird.

A day came when Maria was told she had to have a test that would be the hardest for her. It was to happen later that afternoon.

"We have to get what's called a biopsy," Dr. Seager explained to Maria, me, and her parents. *"We're going to have to take out a tiny bit of your kidney. That will require us to guide a long needle into the area."*

Before the doctor could finish, Maria jumped up from her chair and ran around behind her parents. *"No. No. No more needles. I know it's going to hurt. Daddy, don't let them do it."* She had so many tears, droplets clung to her chin before dropping to the floor.

Her parents almost cried to see Maria so frightened and hurting so much from her illness, yet hurting equally as much from the tests. They spoke softly to her.

"It's the last test," her mother said. *"We know it's the toughest one. We also know how terrified you are. But Teddy is with you. So are we. It will only take a few minutes and then it'll be over. I promise."*

Once Maria stopped sobbing, the doctor went on to explain the procedure. *"There'll be a machine in the room called an ultrasound. There's a little probe we'll put on your skin and it will show your kidney on the screen. It doesn't hurt."*

"Like my kidney is on TV?" Maria asked with a hitch in her voice.

"Yes, like it's on TV. That way we can see exactly where to pinch out the little bit of kidney we need. We'll also put some medicine on your skin where the needle will go. That way it won't hurt very much. But it will hurt a little bit."

"Can't you give me enough medicine so it won't at all? I hate needles."

"I can't because before it hurts too much it will all be over. That's better, isn't it?"

Maria pushed out her bottom lip and scowled. *"None of it's better. Is it the last test, though? Then I can go home? What are you going to do with it anyway?"*

Maria's mother breathed out a volcanic sigh. All of Maria's questions were a signal she was accepting the need for the test.

"We put it on a slide and then look at it under a microscope. We'll be able to

see exactly where things aren't quite right with it."

Maria slumped back in her chair and scowled some more. But she didn't ask any more questions.

The doctor talked more with her parents and then dismissed all of us by saying, *"Go on back to Maria's room. Members of my team will drop by in a few hours to prepare Maria for the biopsy."*

"I tried to be brave," she said to me that night. *"But I'm not brave. I'm just a little kid and all this stuff is scary and bigger than me. And all these strangers are poking at me."* She started to cry. I was happy to be her tissue.

Good Days & Bad Days
Chapter 3

*"**Can I go home now?**"* Maria asked her parents as we walked back to her hospital room.

Her mother kneeled down on one knee. She turned Maria toward her. *"**Not today. You'll stay for a while. When your father and I can't be here, Evie, your nurse, will be. Of course Teddy will be, too.**"*

*"**Am I going to die here?**"* Maria asked the doctor.

I heard Maria's voice go up another level from where it already was. She was breaking apart. Maybe she'd faint right there on the floor. Her mom and dad thought she might not reach her next birthday. That was only a few months away.

*"**I'm afraid,**"* she said. *"**I don't want to die, ever.**"* What else could she say? She was terrified. Would her brain explode from it? Would she have to stay in bed all the time? Could she play if she felt like it? There were so many questions. But right then trembling fear lived inside Maria.

Her mother grabbed Maria around the waist and lifted her up. She kissed Maria all over her face until we got to the room. *"**You're not going to die here,**"* she said repeatedly. *"**I can promise you that much.**"*

As they resettled into Maria's hospital room, the doctor walked into the room and asked everyone to have a seat.

"The test results are all in. Maria has a rare kidney disease. It's a form that doesn't have a cure. We'll try a combination of medications to see if we can help you feel better." He then turned and walked out to talk with the nurse, Evie.

Then Evie popped in carrying a paper cup about the size of a tennis ball, inside was a Thumbelina-sized pill. *"The doctor wants you to take this,"* she said handing Maria the cup.

"What's it for?" Maria asked, still sniffling. She wiped her nose with her forearm.

"It may slow down your kidney disease."

Maria looked at her mother. Then at her father.

Her father said, *"We're counting on it. Go ahead and take it, honey."*

"It might make you sick to your stomach at first," Evie cautioned while pouring Maria a glass of water. *"Getting sick from it is what we call a side effect. It comes from the medicine, not from the disease. When you get used to the medicine, it won't make you sick."*

The side effect stayed with Maria during her whole hospital stay, which was several weeks. When she fell asleep at night, tears ran down her face. Her pillow, and me, were soaked every morning.

Her parents took off work, staying with her as much as possible. On the weekends, since he wasn't in school, Doug came to visit. He brought Maria coloring books and games as well as her favorite books.

The whole family came to celebrate when Maria was finally released. She had plenty of energy to jump off the bed to go home. Doug was just as excited. When he hugged her, he lifted her feet off the ground.

During the ride back to her house, Maria's excitement faded. She thought about all the things that could happen anytime. Would things be different because she was different, now?

She asked her parents, *"Will I go to school? Does everyone know I'm really sick and I might die? Except for Doug? I don't want anyone else to know."* Her voice quivered, holding back more tears.

"Your teachers and the school principal know. If something happens and you feel sicker than you already do, they'll know what to do. Your friends and classmates don't know," her mother said. *"It's up to you if you tell them or not."*

"I don't want to go to school ever again! Everyone will look at me funny like they already do. Except it'll be worse, now."

"You have to go to school. It's the law," said her dad. His tone was more weary than serious.

"It's against the law to die when I'm just a kid, too!"

Maria kicked the seat in front of her. She crossed her arms and sunk her chin to her chest. She muttered, *"Nothing is ever going to be right."*

Every night Maria talked to me all about school and how the kids treated her.

"Jeff was mean. He said I was ugly because my face was so puffy. Miss Lukens told him to stop. He keeps doing it when she's not looking. Other kids look away when they see me. Sometimes I feel like I'm in a bubble. Other times I feel invisible. Nobody likes me anymore." Then she'd gulp in giant tears.

I kept quiet, like I normally did. I'm glad she talked. After talking at night, Maria's mood was up in the morning. But it went down during the day. It was like riding a roller-coaster.

One night Maria didn't talk about school. She talked how she was feeling. *"Teddy, my stomach still hurts, but not from the medicine or my kidney. It hurts because it wants to throw up how scared I feel. I don't want to be sick. I can't die. It's not fair. I'll miss mom and dad. I'll miss Doug. I'll miss Mittens. Mostly I'll miss you."* She kissed each one of my paws. Then my ears. Then my nose.

She talked about dying a lot after that. Her terror about never seeing anyone or anything again was bigger than the whole world. Her heart banged against her chest as if her fear made it beat. Each night when she finished talking, she'd say the same thing before falling asleep. *"At least when I die all this hurting will be over. I'll just fall asleep like Grandpa. When I wake up, I'll be with him."*

The weeks rolled into months. The short, six-month the doctors had told Maria's parents grew closer. The family was skittish hoping Maria wouldn't die that soon. Nevertheless, things seemed better. Maria had more energy, which meant the medicine was doing its job. Pretty soon they were counting the days until Maria's tenth birthday.

"We're throwing you the biggest party ever," her mother told her. *"Everyone will be there. You'll get lots of presents and I'll make your favorite cake, chocolate with chocolate frosting. You can have chocolate ice cream, too."*

I don't ever have a big party, Maria thought. *"It's because I'm going to die, isn't it?"* Her face didn't move when she asked. There were no tears. Her lips didn't quiver.

I saw her mother gulp down a lump the size of an orange. She lowered herself until she was eye-to-eye with her daughter. *"I'm not going to lie to you. Nothing I can tell you will be worse than what you're dealing with. We're giving you a big party because you have had a tough couple of months. So we're celebrating you."*

Then her mother grabbed Maria so tight Maria was afraid she'd die of suffocation right there. Even so, she felt safe and very loved. It didn't change anything, but she felt better anyway.

Party day arrived loaded with balloons and glitter. Her friends and all the members of her family, even her aunts and uncles, attended. Presents towered on the table. For a few hours everyone forgot Maria was so very sick.

In the days following the party, the mood in the house shifted. No one talked about the upcoming doctor's appointment even though everyone knew there'd be more tests than usual. Those tests would reveal how well the medicine was really working. They would also tell them if Maria would live longer than the doctor believed. We all tiptoed as if we were on a tightrope. If the tests told us Maria had more time to live, we'd fall off the tightrope to the right. They could say she'd die soon. If so, we'd fall off the tightrope to the left. If we fell to the left, we would want to die, too.

I went with her for all those tests. We waited for the results together.

Then came the best news ever! The test results were good!

The doctor said, *"The medicine has slowed down the progression of the disease. It's not gone. However, it's not worse. That's good news."* His smile glittered.

Relieved laughter filled the entire room. There was so much happiness at the news, it almost spilled into the streets. We sort of ignored the part that the kidney disease wasn't gone.

The night we got the good news, Maria sat up in her bed. She drew her knees to her chest and sat me on top of them.

"Since the medicine works, maybe I'll have an eleventh birthday party. Maybe I won't die at all. Do you think the medicine will get rid of it forever?"

I didn't know any answers. I hoped her parents talked to her about hoping for things so big. I remembered the doctor said the disease wasn't gone. But the longer Maria was with us, the easier it was to believe it had vanished.

With each passing month, Maria and her parents relaxed. But I noticed Maria was more serious than she used to be. She didn't laugh as much. She didn't smile as much. She was quieter. She escaped into her books more than she used to. She still liked the stories, but stopped talking about having adventures when she was all grown up. She gave up a lot of the dreams we had chased around in the woods before all this began.

Knowing in her heart she was going to die, but not exactly when, changed her into a somber little girl. I was more serious, too.

Then one day she brought home a new friend.

"Teddy," Maria said, *"This is Lynn. She's my new best friend. At least my new best human friend. Today we're going to give all the kitties a bath! You're coming with us!"*

She grabbed my arm and the three of us went racing around the house to gather up six kittens.

"We'll put them all in the carriage," she called to Lynn when she wheeled it out of a side room.

I got thrown into the carriage first. Then the two girls scrambled searching for kittens. As they located each one, they plopped it in on top of me. I didn't like that very much. Plus, their mewing drove me crazy. If I could have, I'd have said, *"Giving six kittens a bath is a very bad idea. Stop now."*

It took a while to fetch all the kittens. The minute they plunked one into the carriage, another one would jump out. Finally the girls gave up the idea of wheeling them into the bathroom in the carriage. Instead they'd push one inside then slam the door shut so it wouldn't escape. Then they'd chase down another one until all six of them were locked in the bathroom along with the girls and me.

Once we were all housed inside the tiny room, the girls filled the white bathtub with warm water while I sat on a towel watching.

"*It's deep enough,*" said Lynn when it was about a quarter full.

"*Then let's do it!*" said Maria, clapping her hands together. She peered at two kittens scratching at the door. Another two clawed at one another behind the sink.

"*Which one of you will go in first?*" Maria asked. "*I think it should be you.*" She plucked a kitten she called Zoey by the scruff of the neck. The next thing I knew Maria dunked Zoey into the tub.

Lynn dropped Thomas in beside Zoey. Next a kitten named Ginger took the plunge, than another Lucy, and another Shadow. The last kitten, Nikki, was deposited into the water which, by now, looked like ocean waves due to all the kittens splashing.

Mewing turned into a high pitched wail. The kittens tried clawing their way out of the tub. The smooth porcelain of the tub made it impossible for them to grip a single thing.

While the girls squirted shampoo on their fur, the kittens scratched the girls' hands. Zoey climbed on top of Thomas and jumped higher than the tub edge. She landed on Lynn's shirt, crawled up to her shoulder, then down her back.

"*Owie, owie!*" Lynn yelled as Zoey's nails dug through her shirt into her back, tearing it in the process. Finally Maria nabbed Zoey off Lynn and dropped her back into the tub.

Since the bathroom door was closed, when the girls hauled all the kittens out of the bathtub they didn't escape when they ran toward it. It was only then the girls noticed they were soaked. The walls dripped with water as if the shower had been on. The floor was so drenched it would take a million towels to soak it all up. It would take a million more to dry the squirming, wailing kittens.

Then, from outside the door, Maria's mother called, "*I'm home.*" Her shoes clipped down the hallway. When she heard the commotion from the bathroom, she knocked on the door. "*What's going on in there?*"

The doorknob clicked as it turned. As soon as there were a few inches of space, six kittens sprinted past her. Maria and Lynn didn't move. They didn't even breathe.

"*What. Have. You. Done?*" Maria's mother demanded. "*Don't lie to me,*" she said staring at Maria. "*Is this how you behave when you have your friend Lynn here for a visit?*"

Busted.

"*The kittens needed a bath,*" Maria explained, jumbling her words all into

one. "*So we gave them one.*"

"*Kittens don't need baths. This bathroom looks like a flood. Clean it up right now!*" Then she turned on her heels and stomped out.

Maria and Lynn looked at each other. Then at me. Giggles bubbled up through their throats. They laughed so hard, they rolled around in the puddles on the floor. It took an hour to clean up the sopping mess.

Once Lynn went home, Maria's mother gave her a punishment. "*Young lady, you're washing and drying all fifteen of those towels. By yourself. Doug is not allowed to help you, so don't ask him.*" Maria didn't think that was a very big punishment. She nodded her head, and then got busy washing towels.

That night Maria fell asleep without crying or telling me how scared she was. It was the first time since she learned about the kidney disease. Right before she fell asleep she said, "*This was the best day ever.*" My heart shined.

While Maria slept, I heard her mom talking on the phone with her friend. The best thing I heard her mother say was, "*It was hard to give her a big punishment because she was acting like her old self. She was, well, normal again. I've missed that side of her so much.*"

More of Maria's days became like the kitten bath day, only not so wet. She laughed a little more each day. We always tried to forget about the kidney disease, even though deep down we knew it could take Maria away in a second.

Maria's family tended to spoil her by giving her things she asked for. I wondered if Doug got a little jealous. He didn't seem to. He understood she might not get another chance to have certain things, just like her big tenth birthday party. He loved Maria. Once he said, "*I'll do anything for you, sis.*" Then he ruffled her hair.

Maria didn't ask for things very often. She didn't really want to be treated differently. Like most kids, Maria wanted different things at different times. Then she'd forget all about them. Except for one thing she wanted most in the entire world. A dog. She'd never had a dog except when she was really little and she didn't really remember him.

One day her mother came home and called Maria from the front door, "*Maria, come here.*"

"*Mom,*" Maria whined from her room. "*I'm too tired. I have a lot of homework.*"

"*I know you're tired, but I really need your help. It'll only take a few minutes. Then you can get back to your work.*"

I saw Maria roll her eyes even though her mother didn't. "*What?*" Maria said, coming down the stairs.

Then she saw the tip of what looked like a little gray tail. Maria trudged a little faster.

Seconds later a gray jumble of fur jumped up on her. "*A dog?*" Maria hooted. "*A dog? Is it for me?*"

Her mother's golden smile told Maria everything she needed to know.

"*For you,*" Maria's mother said. "*I adopted him from a family here in town. He's about 6 months and his name is Peppy. Peppy the poodle. He's yours to take care of. I'm not taking care of him for you. Understood?*"

Maria nodded her head bobblehead-style. "*Come on, Peppy!*" Maria shouted. "*I'll show you my room. Then I'll introduce you to Teddy.*"

Maria loved Peppy the minute she saw him. I could tell he gave something to Maria I couldn't, even though I wanted to. He gave Maria something to look forward to each day. Something that wasn't burdensome like homework, or enduring more hospital tests. In some ways Peppy gave Maria a reason to get up every morning. That was important to all of us. She fed Peppy. She gave Peppy water. She walked Peppy. From time to time she even gave Peppy treats.

The gray mass of fur never left Maria's side except when she was at school. Even on the days when she didn't feel well at all and did nothing except lie on the couch watching TV, Peppy stayed with her.

Each night Peppy wormed his way down into the covers with Maria. Eventually he'd sleep with his head on the pillow right next to hers. Except for me, Peppy was the best friend Maria ever had.

I wished all of Maria's days were like the kitten bath day, or when she had tons of energy to keep up with Peppy. They weren't. Maria had good days, and terrible days, too. On terrible days she'd whisper to me, "*I think the medicine stopped working.*" On those days she cried rivers of tears. Those were the times she'd admit to me, "*Just let me die and get it over with.*" In those moments nothing made her feel loved and safe. Not me. Not her parents. Not even Peppy.

"*Please let Maria wake up in the morning,*" was the single prayer all of us prayed each night before drifting off to sleep.

Having Hope
Chapter 4

The medication must have helped because Maria woke up every morning.

At the breakfast table Doug teased her before leaving for school. It made Maria feel warm inside.

This was our routine, the new normal. When a year had gone by since we first learned about Maria's illness, we knew the medicine was working better than expected.

At her one-year checkup, Maria's parents couldn't help but ask about it.

"*A prognosis,*" the doctor explained, "*is only an estimate of how long Maria might live. Other factors, like Maria's diet, keeping her blood pressure under control, as well as her attitude can lengthen her time. Of course there are always miracles.*" The disease is in remission.

"*Do you think she'll live another year?*" Maria's father asked.

The doctor scanned Maria's file, took off his glasses and said, "*I don't know. Her medical care is what we call experimental. New things come up all the time. When they do, if I think it can help Maria, I'll talk it over with you. In the meantime, every day is a blessing.*"

"*Will the medicine keep working?*" Maria's mother asked.

The doctor looked up at the corner of the room, thinking. Then he looked back at Maria's parents. "*Yes, the medicine is working. It's keeping the disease in remission. That means it looks the same now as when she started taking it. I'm not saying it's gone.*"

"*How long will she be in remission?*" Maria's parents asked the question of the doctor at the exact same time.

"*There's no timing I can give you on that. It could be weeks. It could be years. That's why we're always bringing her back for tests.*"

Maria turned eleven. Then she was twelve, it seemed like she never had kidney disease. But hospital visits, tests, and check-ups reminded us all the time. So when Maria came back from each one saying, "*So far, so good,*" we were thankful.

Those were the nights Maria's mom always made her favorite foods.

When Maria was going into the fifth grade, her mother remarried and moved to the city called LaCrosse. Even though it was still in Wisconsin, it was too far away for Maria, or Doug, to go to their same school. Or keep their same friends.

Even though Maria was in remission from her kidney disease, her father didn't want to be too far away, but he had a job in Beaver Dam so he stayed on the hobby farm.

Maria's grandparents, who owned their own farm, agreed to take all of the animals. So a week or two before moving day, the whole family helped load up all the animals into special trucks.

The journey to the new farm was confusing to the animals. Once they arrived, though, they seemed to adjust quickly. Maria's grandparents assured her, and Doug, they would take good care of them.

Besides me, the only animal left was Peppy. Not even Mittens came with us.

The new house was larger than the house in Beaver Dam. So there was plenty of room for all of us. Peppy enjoyed his new yard where his favorite game was chasing birds.

"*Do I have to tell my new friends about my kidney disease?*" Maria asked her mother a few weeks into the newest school year.

"*Not if you don't want to. Like always, we told your teachers and the principal. They have to know what to look for. Just in case.*"

Maria made new friends Kay, Susie, Marianne, and Cathy just to name a few. She even signed up for some clubs her new school offered.

One morning about halfway through her fifteenth year, Mary felt a familiar weakness. It was just like how she felt when she'd had to go to the hospital for the first time. She dashed over to her mirror. She pressed on her cheeks. They were swollen. She checked her stomach. Even though her clothes still fit, she could tell it puffed out a little.

Because she was older, Maria didn't carry me around as much as she used to. We were still best friends, though. She stumbled over to where I sat on her pillows and said, "*I think remission might be over. I don't know what to do. Maybe I really am going to die.*"

By now Maria was old enough to understand what dying really meant. Yes, she would go to sleep. No, it wouldn't hurt. But she'd never wake up. She'd come to believe the medicine had gotten rid of the disease. Realizing it hadn't, her heart almost burst out of her chest. Her breath came in spurts. She dug her nails into the palms of her hands.

"*I have so many things I still want to do. I want to live forever,*" she whispered into my ears. "*I guess I'm not going to.*" Tears trickled down her cheeks. "*I'm afraid to tell Mom. But I have to.*"

She shuffled into the kitchen where her mother, as usual, was making breakfast.

"*Mom,*" she said.

"*What is it, honey?*" Her mother kept whisking the eggs.

Maria collapsed on a kitchen chair, folded her arms on the table and sobbed into them. "*I think I'm going to die for real this time.*"

It took her mother one step to reach Maria. "*Settle down. Tell me why you think you're going to die for real this time. The medicine has been working fine. The tests have been great.*"

"*Because it's back,*" she muffled into the crook of her arm.

"*What!*" It wasn't a question. It was a statement of terrorized fear.

When Maria lifted her head to explain, she noticed her mother's otherwise tanned face was pale. It was happening all over. Maria felt isolated from the whole world once again. She was going to die.

In seconds Maria's mother had placed a call to the doctor. He scheduled an appointment that very next day. Maria endured what seemed like millions of tests.

The results confirmed Maria's fear. In spite of how good the medicine had been, and how well Maria had followed all the doctor's orders, the disease was back. Worse than ever.

Because Maria wasn't a little girl any longer, he was blunt. He spoke directly to her. "*You're old enough now to get a kidney transplant. But if a donor match doesn't come up soon enough, you will need to go on dialysis as there's nothing else we can do.*"

Changing Times
Chapter 5

"*Isn't there anything else we can do?*" Maria's mother asked Dr. Dahlberg. The tone of his voice sounded like she was on her knees begging for a miracle.

Maria's mother simply sat, head bowed, with her fingertips pressed to her eyes.

"*For one thing, make sure you follow her kidney diet perfectly. Low protein and no salt. And you, young lady,*" he looked directly at Maria as if he could see into her soul, "*are to limit how much you drink every day. Each drink of water forces your kidneys to work. So no more than four small glasses a day. Including milk.*" He held up the palm of his hand and pointed to it with the other. "*When I say 'small' I mean half the size of my hand.*"

Maria nodded.

The doctor cleared his throat. "*Now that she's older,*" he explained, "*we can put her on dialysis. Do you know what that means, Maria?*"

"*No, sir.*"

"*What we do is hook you up to a machine. It cleans poisons out of your blood for you. Like your kidneys would naturally do.*"

"*Does it hurt?*" Maria asked.

"*A needle is inserted into your arm. It might pinch a little at first. After awhile it stops hurting. Since needles bother you, we can give you a little numbing medicine before using them. The good news is, you don't have to wear one of our paper nighties. You can keep your own clothes on. Bring one of your adventure books to read. Each dialysis session takes a little over four hours. You'll finish a lot of books since you have to be here three times a week.*"

Maria jumped up, nearly dropping me. "*What about my school activities? I'll miss them.*"

No one said anything.

Maria's mother reached around her waist and tugged her close. "*Sweetie, we'll figure out something. But you're going to have do this. Ask yourself what's more important. Your activities now, or the possibility of doing lots of things later?"*

Maria plopped down in her chair so hard it almost tipped backwards. *"This isn't fair! I hate my life like this!"*

Again, no one said anything. Since Maria sat between her parents, they both leaned in toward her and squeezed her together. They stayed glued to each other for what seemed like hours.

Maria's mother broke away first and stood up as a signal it was time to go. The doctor rose next saying, *"I'm so sorry. These things are never easy."*

I know Maria felt like punching him. She felt like punching everyone and everything. A big, fat tear rolled down her pale cheek. She sniffled it away.

"My receptionist will set up your dialysis schedule. See her before leaving." The doctor closed his folder as we shuffled out of his office.

The receptionist put Maria on a Monday, Wednesday, Friday rotation. The first treatment was Monday, only a few days away.

When Maria walked into the kitchen for breakfast that Monday morning, she said, *"Mom, what does ammonia taste like?"*

"I don't know. Why?"

"It's all I taste anymore. At least I think it's what ammonia tastes like. Ammonia smells like what I have in my mouth all the time."

Her mother nodded. *"It's because your kidneys aren't working right. The dialysis will help. Then maybe your appetite will come back. You're getting too thin."*

"Will it make my skin less yellow and puffy?" Maria asked, looping a strand of hair behind her ear.

"A little. It won't take it all away, though."

"Figures."

Maria was more angry than sad. It seemed like she wasn't Maria anymore. She was a sick kid who was missing her whole life. Everyone else was going to sleep over's, eating potato chips, playing basketball and giggling about cute boys. Anything she did could trigger a relapse. She didn't stay over at anyone's house because she couldn't eat a regular meal. She was ashamed and embarrassed. She was sick and tired of being different.

So when they got to the hospital and she saw the dialysis machine, she wanted to tear it apart. It was about the size of a vending machine and had tons of wires connected to it. On one side stood a tall pole with hooks on the top. Maria had been in the hospital enough times to know what one of those meant they'd hang a bag of liquid medicine from it. The medicine would come out of it through a little tube straight into her body. On the front of the machine was a computer screen. Maria knew the information running across one of those told the doctors and nurses what was going on between her body and the machine.

When no one was looking she kicked it a little. When it moved she was terrified she'd broken it. Then she saw it was on wheels.

She climbed onto the big, tan lounge-type chair next to the machine. She closed her eyes as they attached the tubes to her arm. A nurse flipped a switch and the lengthy ordeal began.

"*It's six hours out of my day,*" she whined to Doug when she got home. "*Six whole hours! It's my whole day. My whole life! Plus I'm sicker to my stomach now than I was before.*"

Doug, who was now twenty-one, had come right over to the house when Maria had called him.

"*I just don't think I can do this.*" Maria buried her head into his shoulder as they sat together on the living room couch.

He held her tight, then said, "*I know the dialysis can make you feel sick. After you get used to it, that side effect will go away. Beyond that, tell me what's scaring you.*"

Maria pulled away. "*I didn't say I was scared.*"

He shook his head. "*No, kiddo. You're scared.*"

"*You don't know everything.*" She stuck her tongue out at him.

"*You're right,*" he said nodding. "*I don't. But I know you.*" He ruffled her hair. "*I'm not leaving until you tell me.*"

"*You mean what scares me besides dying*?" Her voice quivered the same way her bottom lip did.

"*Besides that. What else*?"

"*There's nothing scarier.*"

"*Maybe not. You're scared of more, though. Trust me. There's more. Now, think. Really think.*"

She bit her bottom lip. The clock on the wall ticked as she forced her brain to come up with an answer.

"*Don't use your head. Use your heart for the answer.*" Doug cocked his head toward her, encouraging her honest response.

Finally she threw her head into Doug's lap and sobbed enough tears to fill the Atlantic Ocean. Through the tears she said in muffled tones.

"*I won't get to read any more books. I won't see any more animals. No more fun. No more movies. I won't see my friends any more. No more bikes or football games. Not even a senior prom. No more. . .no more anything! No more you! I won't even get to see my nieces and nephews, if I ever have any. I won't even be able to get married!*"

Her list went on forever. If she wrote it on paper, it might circle the whole world.

"*It's the life you might not have that's the worst, then.*" Doug said. It was a statement rather than a question.

He didn't have to say anything else for Maria to know he understood.

They talked a little more. Eventually Maria said, "*It's been a long day. I'm really tired. I'm going to bed, okay? Thanks.*"

Doug kissed her on top of her head and said, "*As you wish, Princess Maria. As you wish.*" Then he bowed.

She giggled and punched him in the arm. Then she dragged her weary, broken body down the hallway to her bedroom.

As Doug watched her go, he made a decision. He had to check out a few things before he shared it with everyone. If it worked out, it was a decision that would impact all of them in a major way.

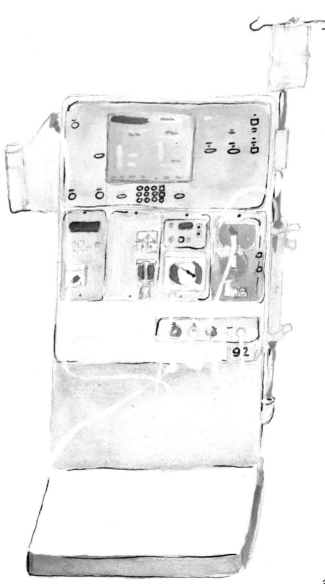

Grateful
Chapter 6

Over the years Doug had kept up with the new treatments for kidney disease. Things could be done that weren't available when Maria was first diagnosed. The one he was most interested in was the kidney transplant. It was new, but recommended more and more.

He knew Maria was going on a donor list. However, a donor might not be available fast enough. So he asked Maria's doctor to see what could be done to get her to the top of the list.

He was still sorting through everything he'd learned when his mother asked him if he could take Maria to her dialysis appointment. He agreed. When he saw his little sister hooked up to the dialysis machine he knew what he needed to do. He knew what he wanted to do. If he could help it, she wasn't going to be linked to the metal monster for the rest of her life.

He called a family meeting. Of course I was included in this meeting because I'd been with Maria during her whole kidney disease journey. I didn't know what to expect since family meetings didn't usually mean good news.

When everyone was assembled around their mother's kitchen table, Doug wasted no time getting to the point.

"*I'm donating a kidney to Maria.*"

Everyone stared at Doug.

"*What?*" said their mother. "*That's still a newer procedure. We don't know anything about it.*"

"*Wrong,*" said Doug. "*I've done my homework. A person can live fine with one kidney.*" He smiled at Maria. "*Then we can both live normal lives.*"

Maria's mother shook her head. "*No, I can't let you do that. There are risks.*"

"*The bigger risk is Maria dying,*" said Doug. "*None of us want that.*"

"*What if you die, too?*"

"*I'm not going to die, Mom. It'll be fine.*" He grinned a little boy grin that had gotten him out of so many punishments. "*I'm healthy.*"

"*I agree with your mother. It's too new. It's too experimental,*" his wife Kathy said.

Doug took a deep breath. "*I've already spoken with the doctor in Madison and I am going to be tested. My decision is made. I'm twenty-one and you can't stop me.*"

Just like the day they found out about Maria's kidney disease, the oxygen in the room disappeared. Hope and terror existed together in the little kitchen.

Maria sprang from her chair and wrapped her arms around her brother's neck. *"You'd do this for me?"*

"If you don't stop squeezing my neck, I won't."

The two laughed some of the terror out of the room.

The family talked for hours after Doug's big announcement. They fought a little. They cried a little. They talked a lot.

At one point Doug said, *"Come on. It's not a big deal."*

"It is a big deal!" Maria said. *"It's a huge deal. What if something happens to you and you need your extra kidney?"*

"Nothing is going to happen to me. Stop worrying." Doug sounded exasperated. *"My mind is made up. This discussion is over. Maria needs a normal life. This solves everything."*

They all looked at each other across the table. They silently agreed it wasn't a perfect solution. But it was the best solution available.

At the same time they said, *"Okay. What do we do now?"*

After Doug explained he would get tested and if he was a match, the transplant operation would be set up. Maria asked him, *"Are you sure, really sure, you want to do this?"*

"I'd do almost anything for you, Sis."

With that, it was settled.

The transplant was scheduled for October 7, 1980, at The University of Wisconsin Hospital. While Doug and Maria were being prepared for it, we were shown a surgical waiting room. We'd wait here while they were in surgery. The room had green, fake leather chairs with steel arms. The floor was white with black flecks on it. There were lamps providing light no brighter than the moon. Maybe it was so no one could see the fear and sadness on people's faces. Maria's mother gripped me like Maria always did. Doing so brought comfort to her the same way it did for Maria.

"What if they both die?" Maria's mother said as the last nurse stepped through a set of doors taking her children into the operating room. The doors between her, Doug, and Maria had a big red sign on them. Etched in white letters were the words Employees Only.

"We can't dwell on that. Let's stay positive. He's young and healthy. Dr. Belzer wouldn't have allowed it otherwise. We both know this is Maria's only chance. I'm proud of them both."

The surgery lasted about six hours. A nurse came out periodically and let us know how things were going. She said the same thing every time. *"They're doing fine. It's going well."* Between her announcements, we held our breaths. After each announcement we exhaled.

The parents paced. Her friends looked terrified. They all flipped through outdated magazines without reading a word. For a little while they went to the chapel and prayed. I did, too.

When Dr. Belzer finally came out, Maria's mom and dad jumped from their chairs. They raced toward him almost knocking him down.

"How's Maria? Doug? Are they alright? Is everything good? They're alive?"

The questions burst out like fireworks. The doctor waited until they'd run out of them before he spoke.

"They're great. We're very hopeful that Maria's body will accept Doug's kidney. As far as Doug, he'll be fine."

Six weeks after the surgery, Doug resumed his life as if nothing had happened. He even went hunting with his buddies.

As for Maria, her body accepted Doug's kidney. Little by little she relearned how to live a normal life. More importantly, she once again believed she'd see the sun rise through her bedroom window every morning. Doug had given her more than a kidney. He'd given her light, hope and a future.

Over the weeks and months following the transplant, Maria struggled with a way to thank her brother for such a personal sacrifice. It was one of her books that gave her the idea of a perfect gift for him.

When she finished writing the poem she had it engraved on a plaque, and handed it to him, her eyes were filled with happy tears. In a whisper she said, *"You'll always be my Super Hero. I love you."*

Doug opened the box she'd given him and read it aloud.

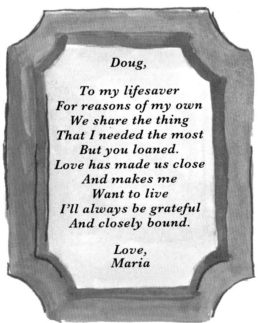

Doug,

To my lifesaver
For reasons of my own
We share the thing
That I needed the most
But you loaned.
Love has made us close
And makes me
Want to live
I'll always be grateful
And closely bound.

Love,
Maria

Today Maria is an adult and married. She doesn't need me any more. But she keeps me around because I was with her through it all.

I'm proud of Doug. I'm proudest of my darling girl, Maria.

All of you reading this story are just as brave as her. So grab your own Teddy and take your own journey one step at a time, just like Maria.

Made in the USA
Lexington, KY
11 July 2018